THE INVISIBLE PORTAL OF MONEY

Shine C. George

Table of Contents

FOREWORD:

In the journey toward understanding wealth and prosperity, we often find ourselves navigating through visible avenues—budgets, investments, and financial strategies. Yet, there exists an unseen realm, an ethereal portal where the true essence of abundance resides. 'The Invisible Portal of Money' masterfully penned by Shine C George opens this gateway, inviting readers into a realm where the intangible forces of wealth converge.

Through this captivating narrative, George sheds light on the elusive nature of financial abundance, guiding us beyond the surface of monetary transactions to the depths of our beliefs, behaviors, and aspirations. With profound insight and compelling wisdom, this book becomes a torchbearer, illuminating the path toward a richer understanding of wealth—one that transcends numbers and embraces the core values that shape our financial destinies.

Prepare to embark on a transformative journey, where the invisible becomes tangible, and the portal to true prosperity beckons. Shine C George's 'The Invisible Portal of Money' stands as an empowering beacon, offering not just knowledge, but the keys to unlock the hidden treasures of wealth within ourselves.

Warm Regards,

(Shine C. George)

INTRODUCTION

The Invisible Portal of Money" is a captivating exploration into the hidden dynamics and psychology behind wealth. Authored by (Shine C. George), this insightful book delves into the unseen forces that shape our relationship with money, offering a unique perspective on how individuals can navigate the complexities of finance. Through compelling anecdotes and practical insights, the book unveils the often-overlooked aspects of abundance, guiding readers toward unlocking their potential to attract wealth and abundance into their lives. Blending personal finance with a deeper understanding of human behavior, "The Invisible Portal of Money" is a thought-provoking read that empowers readers to transform their financial reality by harnessing the unseen pathways to prosperity.

CHAPTER 1

Opening the portal to the invisible Realm of Wealth

Just beyond what your eyes can see, there is a very real spirit world. This unseen realm is responsible for many everyday happenings both good and bad. This is why it's vital for you to understand how to activate the seer anointing and begin seeing into the spirit realm.

Building wealth starts with making a financial plan. That means taking the time to identify your goals and game out how you can accomplish them. Plenty of people dread the "b" word, but budgeting is a key plank in your wealth building strategy. Building a budget and sticking to it helps increase your chances of carrying out your plan and achieving your financial goals. When the furnace goes out or the refrigerator quits working, where does the money come from if you don't have emergency savings? Lori Gross, financial and investment advisor at Outlook Financial Center says credit cards bear the brunt and cause you to incur extra costs and fees, like sky-high interest rates.

By building an emergency fund, you can protect your credit as well as reap the benefits of earning interest on an online savings account all the while enjoying the peace of mind of knowing you have money in the bank to cover life's surprises.

Budgets also help you understand where your money goes each month and prevent behaviors that can endanger your goals, like overspending. Not all debt is created equal and some, like mortgages, may even be considered "good" debt, thanks to their general low interest rates and wealth building potential. Some experts even think of a mortgage payoff as a type of forced savings account because you'll likely see at least a portion of your monthly payment back when you sell.

But if you're rolling over a lot of bad debt, like high-interest credit card bills, every month, you may jeopardize your financial goals. That's why it's important to have a plan for your repayment, Gross says, with the ultimate goal of having a debt-free life. While it isn't a move that you can make at an online brokerage, investing in yourself by raising your income is an important step when it comes to how to build wealth. The more you earn over your lifetime, the more money you have available to invest.

"If you've been living comfortably on your current salary and you receive an increase, this is the perfect opportunity to begin the path to building wealth," says Morgan, whether that means contributing more toward your retirement savings, paying down debt or bumping up your emergency fund savings,

In fact, I recommend you save at least half of every raise you get to position yourself for a secure retirement. This allows you to improve your quality of life gradually while also ensuring you don't fall victim to standards of living that will be impossible for you to maintain in retirement.

Building wealth from nothing requires taking a deep look at your current situation. Evaluate your spending and income for the last several years. Where can you ruthlessly cut your spending? How can you increase your income? Depending on where you're starting from, this may seem impossible and require out of the box thinking.

It's easier to cut luxuries when you're already spending on luxuries to begin with. If you lead a bare-bones existence, you may have to make radical decisions. Find where you can create room in your budget and invest the difference between what you spend and what you earn. Sensible investing over time is one of the easiest ways to grow wealth.

*Understanding the mysterious Nature of Money

Money makes us both master and slave. Our power over money is real

only inasmuch as we are able to understand its power over us.

Man has sought to understand the essence of money for many centuries. Philosophers and economists, statesmen, writers, even poets have written about money. Money has been lauded and cursed, it has been dreamed of and disdained. What is money - good or evil? It brings stability and instability and makes people looking for and running away from it. Money is capable of creating and destroying, of uniting and disuniting. It makes people partners and rivals and can influence the fate of individuals and whole nations. But what does money bring - freedom or dependence? People obtain money working hard and playing and spend it with joy and sadness. Man makes money, and money makes man; it forms his way of living and his way of thinking.

Money is capable of invoking the whole range of emotions. If one could bring together everything that has been written about money at various times and by various nations, one would have a gigantic multicolored canvas of human thoughts and feelings, on which bright and dark tones will alternate, but which will nevertheless retain 'void areas' of the unknown.

Money as the object of cognition enter the realm of a special branch of knowledge, economic science, which, like every other science, has its own subject matter, methods of inquiry and pursues its own goals.

Money is shaped by emotion, trust, relationships and politics. It defies and confounds even experts and financial insiders in their attempts to understand the nature of money and control its behaviour. Money is top of everyone's mind these days. High inflation rates make your money worth less. And high-interest rates to fight inflation make your money more expensive.

It's no wonder that money is such a preoccupation and source of stress. It's one of the strongest, most pervasive forces in our lives. Simply being a participant in modern life requires money: almost everything we do is directly or indirectly mediated by money.

Money conscientiously caters to both the destructive and the constructive actions of man, and is only a means for exercising his will and mind. But in this role money is not passive. It either creates or destroys man himself as a personality, it exerts a strong influence on the building up of his individual system of values and on the alignment of his personal priorities and goals. Everything depends on the correlation between two forces 'reason and money interest' in the purposeful activity of people.

Money is a social good, and society is responsible for its own. Just as once, long ago, money was created by social will, now we must use the strength of social reason in order to understand the place and role of money in the life of society and learn to control this 'atomic force'. This can be achieved by combining the efforts of practically oriented economic science and philosophy striving to cognize the world as a whole.

The philosophy of money is the mode of the intellectual inquiry of the essence of money as a social phenomenon and its influence on the inner world of the individual.

The philosophy of money can make a certain contribution to educating humanity and help people to

**remember that the amount of all
things must always be the man.**

Chapter 2
The Perception of Wealth

The Illusion of Abundance: How Perception Shapes Wealth Reality is truth

Reality, however, is not always a known, which is where perception of reality comes in. While reality is a fixed factor in the equation of life, perception of reality is a variable.

When it comes to your company's costs, perception is reality. About 73% of people say that the reputation of a company or product can impact their decision to buy or not to buy. Before buying, about 60% of consumers conduct some research online and 44% of those read online reviews and opinions. 4 out 5 consumers will reverse their decision based on reviews they read online.

How clients view you is everything, and consistency is key! Brand management is something you need to take seriously from day one and throughout the life of your event, venue or service.

All initiatives, events and marketing campaigns should align with your overall mission and vision. Everything from your website, to social media, to event setup should reflect what you're about.

You've probably heard it said that a happy customer only influences a **handful** of others, while an unhappy customer will influence dozens about a negative experience they had with your event, venue or service. One of the best things you can do for brand management is to offer excellent and fast customer service. If a customer has a problem, apologize and fix it as quickly as possible. Perceived wealth looks only at assets and more the material assets. Actual wealth is a better reflection because it removes the liabilities to attain that wealth. The net worth statement is a great benchmark for actual wealth.

Money can come with lots of negative connotations. But you get to choose how you perceive earning, spending, saving, and investing your cash. If you feel negative about your finances, you can make a change! Changing your perception of money to a positive mindset can help you attain financial success.

The first thing you need to do is get rid of a scarcity mindset related to money, if any. The scarcity mindset is one where you look at money as something limited and hard to get. If you are one of those who continuously worries that you will run out of money, then you fall into this category.

With this mindset, you feel anxious about spending money and struggle to make financial decisions confidently.

The biggest problem with this mindset is that people with it avoid investments and miss opportunities for growth. They will park all their money in savings accounts or fixed deposits. If you have a scarcity mindset, you have a problem to solve, a serious one. However, if you have an abundance mindset, it is a big positive for you. It will help you achieve financial success. An abundance mindset is characterized by the belief that opportunities are abundant and there's enough wealth to go around.

Those with an abundance mindset are likely to take calculated risks, invest wisely, and make informed financial decisions. They see setbacks as temporary and believe they can overcome challenges to achieve their financial goals. This positive mindset promotes a positive relationship with money and encourages the pursuit of opportunities for growth and expansion.

For you to move your money mindset from negative to positive, Recognize your current money mindset and any negative beliefs you hold about money. While evaluating, be true to yourself, as no one will judge you. Awareness is the first step toward change. Unless you acknowledge it, you won't move on to the next step.

Use positive affirmations to rewire your thoughts. Repeat statements like "I attract wealth and abundance" daily to reinforce a positive money mindset. You may build a positive mindset by following whatever strategy you are comfortable with.

Cultivate gratitude for the money you have and the opportunities you encounter. Gratitude shifts your focus from lack to abundance.

Invest time in learning about personal finance, investing, and wealth-building. Knowledge empowers you to make informed decisions.

Surround yourself with individuals who have a healthy money mindset. If you discuss your money matters with people with a scarcity mindset, your positive mindset can change to a negative one. Irrespective of your current mindset status, you need to surround yourself with people with an abundance mindset, as their attitudes can influence your thinking and behavior

Chapter3

Unveiling The Unconscious Relationship With Money.

The Subconscious Mind and Financial Decision Making

Most people believe that sheer force of will and self-discipline are all they need to make better money decisions. However, neuroscience demonstrates that that is not true. So powerful, influential, and hard to govern is our unconscious mind that, if we fail to understand it, we will make mistakes with our money repeatedly.

Your subconscious is always seeking to protect you from perceived danger. It pushes you to stay in the same circumstances; even if they don't serve you because it feels safer, and you're likely afraid to take chances and risk failure. Additionally, your subconscious will fight to keep you from doing things that go against it. Making big life changes that contradict your subconscious beliefs about money may trigger a lot of fear. For instance, if you subconsciously think wealth is bad and you're offered a high-paying job, you might be afraid to take it even if there's no obvious risk involved.

You're likely unaware that your subconscious views exist. This means that your subconscious gets to control your behavior unnoticed, preventing you from growing and changing. Unless you become aware of your subconscious beliefs, you may continue acting against your conscious

The Invisible Portal of Money | Unveiling The
Unconscious Relationship With Money.

25

beliefs without knowing why or how to stop.

For instance, suppose you have a conscious view that you want to save money and invest it in a profitable venture. However, your subconscious view is that money is the root of all evil and that wealthy people are greedy and selfish. As a result, you may find yourself sabotaging your own efforts to save money and invest it without realizing why.

It's difficult for us to accept that we're responsible for bad things that happen to us or to other people. Therefore, the subconscious makes us feel like bad situations are something happening to us instead of something we're causing. For example, if you never have enough money to put away in your savings, your subconscious may tell you that it's because you're unlucky and life is too expensive. In reality, your subconscious is helping you avoid the hard truth that you spend your money on unnecessary things, like streaming services you don't use or countless dinners out.

Start teaching your subconscious mind to obey your list consists of decisions you will make that will let you achieve your dreams. Unfortunately, the unruly unconscious mind will do everything it can to distract you and derail your plans. It will continuously find reasons it can't do what you ask. Psychologists know that the subconscious mind suffers from what is known as 'confirmation bias.' It tends to perceive everything that is input in terms of the way you make it feel. Thoughts, observations, and actions you put into your mind throughout the day do make a difference. You can overcome confirmation bias by using simple, positive affirmations throughout the day that trains your brain to enjoy success

The Invisible Portal of Money | Unveiling The
Unconscious Relationship With Money.

27

Emotions, Beliefs, and Their Influence on Financial Behavior

Emotions and beliefs play significant roles in shaping financial behavior. Here's a breakdown of their influence:

Emotions:
  *Fear and Greed; These are primary emotional drivers in financial decision-making. Fear can lead to selling investments during market downturns, while greed can drive risky investments seeking higher returns.
  *Overconfidence: Feeling overly confident about one's abilities can lead to excessive trading or taking on more risk than prudent.
*Loss Aversion: People tend to feel the pain of losses more intensely than the pleasure of gains, leading to conservative decision-making to avoid losses.

The Invisible Portal of Money | Unveiling The Unconscious Relationship With Money.

28

* Anxiety and Stress: Emotional distress can lead to impulsive decisions, such as panic-selling during market volatility.

Beliefs:
    * Risk Perception: Individual beliefs about risk vary widely. Some people are more risk-averse due to their beliefs about financial security, while others are more risk-tolerant.
    *Market Timing: Believing in one's ability to time the market can lead to frequent buying or selling based on predictions, which may not align with market realities.
    * Long-Term vs. Short-Term Thinking: Beliefs about long-term investing versus seeking quick profits can significantly impact financial choices.
    * Financial Literacy and Education: Beliefs about financial concepts and understanding can influence investment choices and risk tolerance.

The Invisible Portal of Money | Unveiling The
Unconscious Relationship With Money.

29

Influence on Behavior:
 * Investment Choices: Emotions and beliefs often determine the assets individuals choose to invest in, such as stocks, bonds, real estate, or alternative investments.

 *Risk Management: These factors can influence risk-taking behavior, affecting portfolio diversification and asset allocation.

 *Decision Timing: Emotional highs and lows can prompt buying or selling decisions that may not align with long-term financial goals.

 *Financial Planning: Emotions and beliefs can impact savings patterns, spending habits, and overall financial planning strategies.

Mitigating Factors:
 *Education: Increased financial literacy can help individuals make more informed decisions and better understand the influence of emotions and beliefs on financial behavior.

* **Advisors and Support Systems:** Seeking advice from financial professionals or having a support system can provide a rational perspective during emotionally charged financial situations.

*Self-Awareness and Emotional Regulation: Being aware of one's emotions and having strategies to manage them can help in making more rational financial decisions.

External Factors:

Media Influence: News, social media, and financial commentary can evoke emotions and shape beliefs, impacting investment decisions.

*Economic Environment: Overall economic conditions, such as recessions or booms, can influence beliefs about risk and returns, affecting investment behavior.

*Cultural and Social Norms: Cultural attitudes toward money, risk, and investing can significantly shape

The Invisible Portal of Money | Unveiling The
Unconscious Relationship With Money.

31

individual beliefs and financial behaviors.

Strategies for Better Decision-Making:
   *Emotional Discipline: Developing emotional discipline and separating emotions from investment decisions can lead to more rational choices.
   *Systematic Investment Plans (SIPs): Setting up automatic investments reduces the impact of emotional highs and lows on investment decisions.
   *Diversification and Asset Allocation: Creating a well-diversified portfolio aligned with long-term goals can mitigate the impact of emotional decisions.
   *Regular Review and Planning: Regularly reviewing financial plans and goals can help in managing emotions during market fluctuations.

Understanding the interplay between emotions, beliefs, and financial behavior is crucial for making sound

The Invisible Portal of Money | Unveiling The Unconscious Relationship With Money.

32

financial choices aligned with long-term goals and risk tolerance.

Chapter 4
Cryptic Economies and Digital Portals

Navigating the Digital Economy

Cryptic Economies refers to informal or shadow economies that operate outside of formal regulations and official oversight. These can involve unreported income, illicit trade, or underground economic activities that aren't easily tracked or regulated.

Embrace digital tools and platforms to streamline processes, improve efficiency, and reach wider audiences. This includes adopting cloud computing, automation, AI, and data analytics to enhance operations and decision-making.
Establishing a strong online presence is crucial. For businesses, this means having user-friendly websites, mobile apps, and utilizing e-commerce platforms. For individuals, it involves managing digital identities and understanding online security.

The digital economy thrives on data, understanding customer behavior through analytics helps in tailoring products/services and making data-driven decisions for businesses. For individuals, data literacy is becoming increasingly important for personal finance and decision-making.

Utilize social media, SEO, content marketing, and targeted advertising to engage with customers effectively. Personal branding and online reputation management are equally crucial in the digital space. With increased digitization comes the need for robust cyber security measures. Protecting sensitive data and respecting user privacy is imperative for both businesses and individuals.

The digital economy has facilitated remote work opportunities, allowing people to work from anywhere with internet access. This flexibility has reshaped work-life balance and opened new job prospects. New skill sets are in demand, including digital literacy, programming, data analysis, and cyber security. Continuous learning and up-skilling are essential to stay relevant in the job market. The rise of platforms and apps has led to the gig economy, offering freelancers and independent contractors opportunities in various sectors like ride-sharing, delivery services, content creation, etc.

The digital economy offers immense opportunities for innovation and collaboration. Partnering with tech companies, startups, and fostering innovation ecosystems can drive growth.

Navigating the digital economy involves embracing technological advancements, adapting to changing consumer behaviors, and addressing challenges through innovation and strategic decision-making. Staying agile and continuously learning is key to thriving in this ever-evolving landscape.

Education is key to navigating the digital economy. Promoting digital literacy, especially among marginalized communities, is crucial for equal participation and opportunity.

The pace of technological change requires constant adaptation. Both individuals and businesses must remain agile and open to learning and adopting new tools, strategies, and technologies

Block-chain Technology: Gateway to a New Financial Frontier

The digital economy has revolutionized payment methods. Mobile wallets, contactless payments, and crypto-currencies are changing how transactions occur. Understanding these options is crucial for businesses and individuals alike.

Financial technology companies are transforming traditional banking and finance. Services like peer-to-peer lending, robo-advisors, and crowd-funding platforms offer alternatives to traditional financial institutions.

Numerous apps and platforms provide budgeting, investment tracking, and financial planning tools. Utilizing these tools can help individuals manage their finances more effectively in the digital age. The digital economy isn't immune to environmental concerns. E-waste, energy consumption from data centers, and the carbon footprint of digital technologies are pressing issues that need attention.

Companies operating in the digital space face increasing pressure to address social and environmental concerns. Consumers and stakeholders are holding businesses accountable for ethical practices and sustainability initiatives. Education is key to navigating the digital economy. Promoting digital literacy, especially among marginalized communities, is crucial for equal participation and opportunity.

The pace of technological change requires constant adaptation. Both individuals and businesses must remain agile and open to learning and adopting new tools, strategies, and technologies.

The digital economy offers unprecedented global market access for businesses of all sizes. Understanding international markets and adapting strategies for diverse audiences is essential for expansion. Operating globally brings challenges related to varying regulations and legal frameworks across different regions. Complying with these regulations while maintaining a global presence requires carefulness.

Chapter 5
Shadows and Light, the Dual Nature of Money

The Underworld of Finance: Dark Money and Its Impact

Shadows represent darkness, mystery, or the unknown, while light symbolizes clarity, illumination, and enlightenment. This duality is often used to depict contrasts between good and evil, truth and ignorance, or knowledge and secrecy.

It's sometimes used to signify the dual nature of existence, where shadows represent the hidden or subconscious aspects of life, while light symbolizes consciousness, awareness, and truth. Shadows can be associated with Carl Jung's concept of the "shadow self," representing repressed or hidden aspects of an individual's personality, while light might symbolize self-awareness and personal growth.

Embracing both shadows and light can signify achieving a balance between opposing forces, accepting one's darker aspects alongside positive attributes to achieve inner harmony. Exploring the shadows within oneself can lead to personal growth and self-awareness. Recognizing both light and shadows in life can foster empathy, understanding, and acceptance of oneself and others.

Understanding that both shadows and light exist in various aspects of life allows for a more nuanced view of situations, relationships, and the world.

Money is an excellent servant but a terrible master, that's why trading your time for money is not the right equation, don't work for it or you will be enslaved involuntarily. And you will lose the one resource that you can't get back. The most precious resource time. Here if you start with a proven plan, the right strategy, you can literally convert decades of struggles into days of achievement.

Again, you ask yourself, how is it that there are self-made millionaires and Billionaires, at such young age, what makes them so different? The truth, they have the right mindset, a better way to understand the money game than you have and for sure they don't have such a negative association with money. There are rules for this money game, and if you know how it works, why it moves in a certain direction, and the basic laws that govern our finical system, you have no limits.

The biggest problem you're solving the more wealthy you can be, and for that, you need to look where nobody other looking, and make a clear board vision solving that billion problems, don't focus on money, focus on what you can do to make people's life easier, where the market is high in demand, for example, there's a lot of industries here crunching due to covid19, well as an entrepreneur with the right mindset you should be able to provide a creative new solution for this industry, creating the new fresh amazon using all these technologies available or a new innovative care service, yeah it not that easy or simple, but you can do it if get the right tools and shift how you seeing the need of the global market, and that market will be awarded you favorably for doing so. You can create a wealth machine by solving millions or billions of people problems. The world for sure will always need more people to solve these new globalization problems, and you can do it.

Illuminating Positive Hidden Wealth: Untapped Resources

Positive hidden wealth can take many forms beyond monetary value. It might manifest as personal talents, kindness, knowledge, or even a network of supportive relationships. Sometimes, these treasures remain concealed due to modesty or simply not recognizing their significance. Bringing them to light often involves introspection, acknowledging strengths, and sharing them with others. Take time to introspect and identify your strengths, talents, and positive attributes. Consider moments where you've received compliments or felt fulfilled.

Embrace your skills and talents, even if they seem small or mundane. Recognize that they contribute positively to your life and the lives of others.

Don't keep your talents hidden. Share them with others through teaching, volunteering, or simply offering your help when needed.

Connect with like-minded individuals who appreciate and encourage your strengths. Collaborating with others can often amplify your abilities.

Invest in learning and self-improvement. Acquiring new skills or knowledge can uncover hidden talents and expand your positive wealth. Cultivate gratitude for the positive aspects of your life. A positive mindset can help you recognize and appreciate your hidden wealth even more. Often, helping others recognize their positive hidden wealth can also help you see yours more clearly.

Maintain a journal to record moments when you feel accomplished, proud, or genuinely happy. Reflecting on these instances can reveal hidden strengths and sources of joy.

Sometimes, our greatest strengths lie dormant because we haven't explored unfamiliar territories. Trying new things can uncover hidden talents or passions.

Ask friends, family, or colleagues for honest feedback about your strengths. Sometimes, others can see qualities in us that we overlook.

Acknowledge and celebrate small achievements. Recognizing even the smallest successes can boost confidence and reveal hidden capabilities. Be kind to yourself during this journey. Embracing your flaws and understanding that they are part of your uniqueness is crucial.

Picture yourself utilizing your strengths and achieving your goals. Visualization can bring clarity and confidence in recognizing your hidden wealth. Connect your strengths and talents with a purpose or cause you deeply care about. Working towards something meaningful often uncovers hidden wealth.

Surround yourself with people who uplift and encourage you. A supportive environment can boost your confidence and help you recognize your strength.

Money is the problem maker and also the problem solver, People who print the money decides the fate of everyone else on the planet. You can be employee, Entrepreneur or an Investor. We all go through a single universal monetary system that has different names in different countries and print different paper called currency which is nothing but a value derived from the commodity our nation holds.

We all heard these terms like million dollar idea, Billion dollar idea, even trillion dollar idea. But do you know what's zillion dollar idea and holds almost every wealth of the planet. That system is called banking, this zillion dollar system. Funds nation to develop, Do war, protect people, Lend them money, Hold their asset and control pretty much everything on the planet and it's been said handful of people from a secret society control this system for the entire planet.

Untapped resources can encompass various aspects of your life.

Consider skills you possess but haven't fully utilized. These could be creative talents, problem-solving abilities, or even organizational skills that could be beneficial in various aspects of life.

Your social circle and professional contacts often hold untapped potential. They might offer opportunities, advice, or collaborations that you haven't explored yet. Efficiently managing time is a resource in itself. Evaluate how you allocate your time and whether there are areas where you could better invest it for personal or professional growth.

Learning is a lifelong process. You might have untapped knowledge or educational opportunities through books, courses, workshops, or online resources that could enhance your skills or broaden your perspective.

Physical possessions or resources that you have but don't fully utilize or leverage. This might include equipment, property, or other assets that could be put to better use.

Your mindset can be an untapped resource. Shifting to a more positive or growth-oriented mindset can unlock potential you never knew you had. Taking care of your physical and mental health can be a resource that's sometimes overlooked. Energy, focus, and creativity often stem from a healthy body and mind.

Define clear goals and objectives for yourself. Then, assess which resources are necessary to achieve these goals. This exercise can help identify which untapped resources to focus on.

Explore educational resources, whether it's through formal education, online courses, workshops, or mentorship programs. Expand your skill set to harness your untapped potential. Actively engage with your network. Attend events, seminars, or networking gatherings to meet new people and discover potential collaborations or opportunities.

Implement strategies like prioritization, time-blocking, or delegation to maximize the use of your time. This will allow you to allocate more time to explore and utilize untapped resources. Practice mindfulness techniques to enhance self-awareness. This helps identify areas of untapped potential and enables personal growth.

Step out of your comfort zone and try new things. Taking calculated risks can lead to discovering hidden talents or untapped opportunities. Invest time in self-care routines, exercise, and healthy habits. A healthier lifestyle often leads to increased energy and mental clarity, tapping into an untapped resource within yourself.

Regularly evaluate your progress and adapt your strategies as needed. What might have been an untapped resource previously might evolve over time, and staying adaptable is key.

About the Author: Shine C George

Shine C George is a visionary author, financial philosopher, and advocate for unlocking the hidden pathways to prosperity. Born into a family with a deep-rooted appreciation for financial literacy and spiritual wisdom, Shine's upbringing instilled in her a fascination with the intricate dance between wealth and consciousness.

With a background in finance and a passion for exploring the metaphysical aspects of abundance, Shine embarked on a transformative journey. Her studies in behavioral economics, health education and spirituality converged, leading her to delve into the uncharted territories of the human psyche's relationship with money.

A prolific writer known for her introspective insights and eloquent prose, Shine C George crafted "*The Invisible Portal of Money*" as a catalyst for a paradigm shift in the way society perceives and attracts wealth. Her book is a culmination of years spent researching the unseen forces that govern our financial destinies, offering readers a profound exploration into the mystical dimensions of monetary abundance.

Shine's mission extends beyond the written word. She is an inspirational speaker, mentor, and guide to countless individuals seeking to transcend

financial limitations and tap into their inherent potential for prosperity. Through her teachings, Shine empowers others to navigate the hidden realms of wealth with clarity, intention, and conscious awareness.